THE SCIENCE BEHIND
BATMAN'S
FLYING MACHINES

by
Tammy Enz

BATMAN created by
Bob Kane with Bill Finger

SCIENCE BEHIND
BATMAN

CAPSTONE PRESS
a capstone imprint

Published by Capstone Press in 2016
A Capstone Imprint
1710 Roe Crest Drive
North Mankato, Minnesota 56003
www.mycapstone.com

STAR36688

Library of Congress Cataloging-in-Publication Data
Names: Enz, Tammy, author.
Title: The science behind Batman's flying machines / by Tammy Enz.
Description: North Mankato, Minnesota : Capstone Press, 2017. | 2017 | Series: DC super heroes. Science behind
   Batman | Audience: Ages 7-10. | Audience: K to grade 3. | Includes bibliographical references and index.
Identifiers: LCCN 2016003653| ISBN 9781515720362 (library binding) | ISBN 9781515720416 (paperback) |
   ISBN 9781515720454 (ebook pdf)
Subjects: LCSH: Airplanes—Design and construction—Juvenile literature. | Aeronautics—Juvenile literature. |
Batman (Fictitious character)—Juvenile literature.
Classification: LCC TL671.2 .E59 2017 | DDC 629.133—dc23
LC record available at http://lccn.loc.gov/2016003653

Summary: Explores the real-world science and engineering connections to the features in Batman's aircraft.

Editorial Credits
Christopher Harbo, editor; Hilary Wacholz, designer; Wanda Winch, media researcher;
Tori Abraham, production specialist

Artwork by Luciano Vecchio and Ethen Beavers

Photo Credits
Library of Congress: Prints and Photographs Division, 7; NASA: Artwork by Steve Lighthill, 9; Shutterstock:
Chris Parypa Photography, 8, MO_SES_Premium, 6; U.S. Air Force, 15 (left), Staff Sgt. Bennie J. Davis III, 21,
Staff Sgt. Brian Ferguson, 17; U.S. Marine Corps photo by Cpl. Garry J. Welch, 14; U.S. Navy photo, 13, Mass
Communications Specialist 2nd Class Brian Morales, 12, Mass Communications Specialist Seaman Timothy A.
Hazel, 18, MC3 Mark El-Rayes, 11 (top), Photographer's Mate 3rd Class Joshua Karsten, 19; Wikimedia: Bernd.
Brincken, 11 (bottom)

Printed in China.
007727

TABLE OF CONTENTS

INTRODUCTION

SUPER HERO WINGS

The Caped Crusader commands the skies. With his Batplane and Batcopter, Batman tracks down super-villains in the most challenging places. From **supersonic** flight to **vertical** takeoffs, his flying machines are packed with amazing features. Best of all, many real aircraft have these features too.

supersonic—faster than the speed of sound
vertical—straight up and down

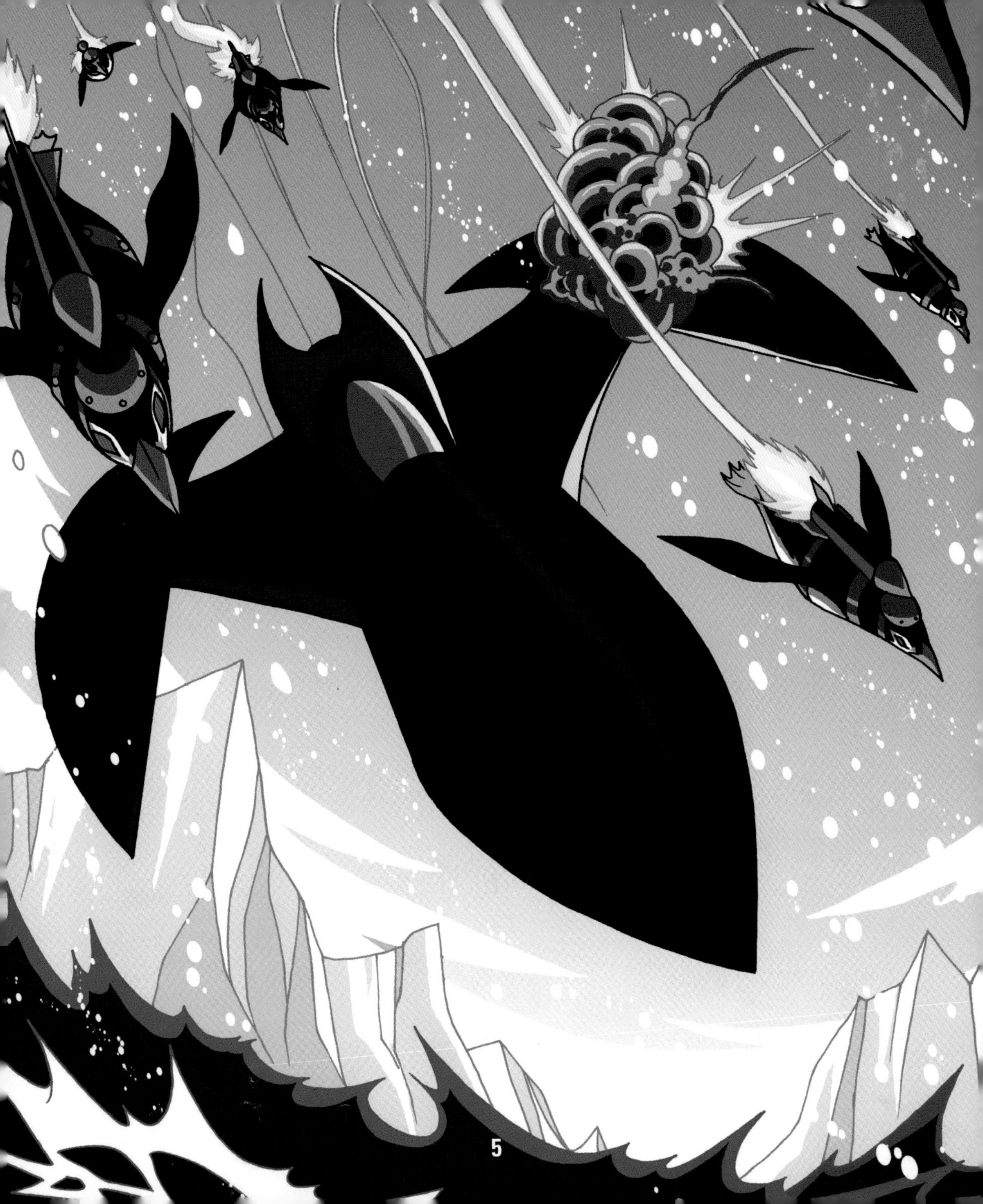

CHAPTER 1
FLIGHT PERFORMANCE

The Batplane uses the same science as real aircraft. Airplane wings are round on the front and **tapered** on the back. Their shape allows air to flow faster over the top than underneath. This air movement creates **lift** to push planes skyward.

In the 1890s, German engineer Otto Lilienthal
built gliders inspired by the shape of bird wings.

taper—to become narrower at one end

lift—the upward force of air that causes an object to fly

The Dark Knight uses the Batplane's powerful jets to chase down criminals. Real jet engines burn fuel to release rapidly expanding gases. These gases then create **thrust** to push planes forward. Some jet engines provide enough thrust to fly faster than the speed of sound.

An F-18 Super Hornet creates a vapor cone as it breaks the speed of sound.

NASA's X-43A holds the record as the world's fastest aircraft. It reached a speed of nearly 7,000 miles (11,265 kilometers) per hour.

thrust—the force that pushes a vehicle forward

To fly in tight areas, Batman uses the Batcopter's **rotor** power.

rotor—a set of rotating blades that lifts an aircraft off the ground

Most helicopters in our world have two sets of rotors. The main rotor on top creates lift. The smaller rotor on a helicopter's tail provides balance. Without balance a helicopter would spin out of control.

Spinning rotors allow an MH-60 Seahawk helicopter to hover above a ship's deck.

FACT

The Eurocopter X3 has two small rotors on its sides instead of its tail. These rotors make it more stable and faster than most helicopters.

CHAPTER 2
AMAZING ABILITIES

The Batplane takes off and lands on the shortest of runways. Some real fighter jets take off and land on very short aircraft carrier runways. A **catapult** helps fling jets off the ship for quick takeoffs. The jets use tail hooks to catch a cable for short landings.

An F-16 Super Hornet catches a cable to land on an aircraft carrier.

FACT

The Navy catapulted its very first aircraft off the USS *North Carolina* on November 5, 1915.

catapult—a device used to launch airplanes from the deck of a ship

No runway at all? That's no problem for the Batplane. It can take off and land similar to a Harrier Jump Jet. This fighter plane's jets fire downward for vertical takeoffs and landings. Once in the air, the pilot changes the angle of the jets for normal flight.

A night-vision camera captures the vertical thrust of the Harrier Jump Jet.

FACT

In the 1950s, the Ryan X-13 Vertijet was designed to launch from a submarine. It could take off and land on its tail.

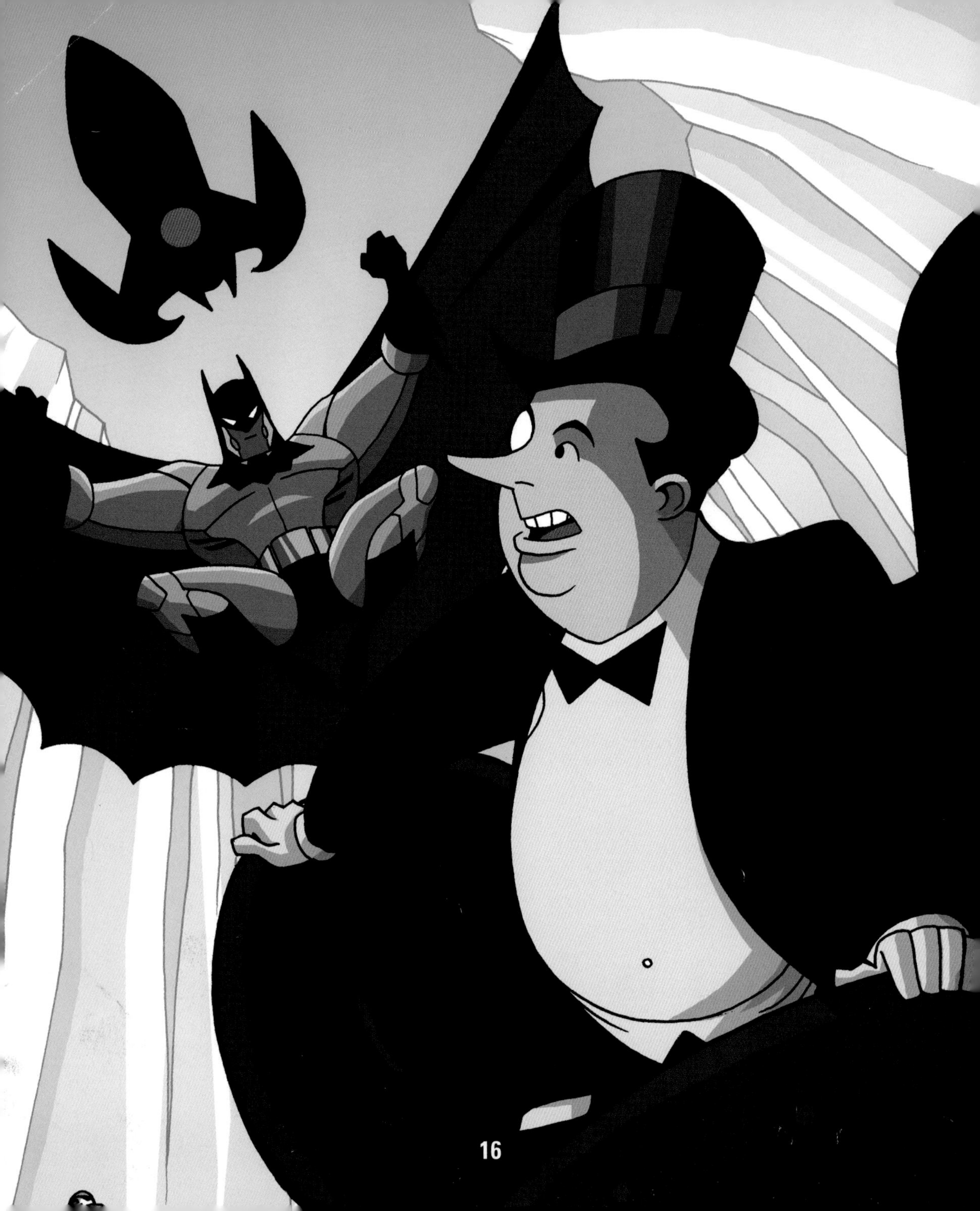

Batman's aircraft sometimes fly without a pilot at all. The U.S. military has more than 10,000 unmanned aircraft. One of them is the MQ-9 Reaper combat drone. It can lock onto moving targets from 50,000 feet (15,240 meters) above Earth.

An MQ-9 Reaper drone comes in for a landing.

CHAPTER 3
ENGAGING ENEMIES

A sailor checks a Sidewinder heat-seeking missile.

Batman's flying machines use **precise** missiles to disarm enemy aircraft. Many military fighter jets carry heat-seeking missiles. These missiles lock onto the heat produced by enemy aircraft. The Sidewinder heat-seeking missile can fly 10 miles (16 km) to reach its target.

Smart bomb

Guided missiles and bombs are called "smart bombs." They are programmed or steered to destroy specific enemy targets.

precise—very accurate or exact

Batman's aircraft use **stealth** mode to catch villains off guard.

stealth—having the ability to move secretly

radar—a device that uses radio waves to track the location of objects

The B-2 Spirit bomber also flies with stealth. Its flat shape and sharp angles make it invisible to enemy **radar**. Its engines also have noise shields. The B-2 can fly close to enemies without being heard.

B-2 Spirit bomber

Batman's aircraft command the skies with state-of-the-art features. The real world science behind them is as amazing as the Caped Crusader himself.

GLOSSARY

catapult (KAT-uh-puhlt)—a device used to launch airplanes from the deck of a ship

lift (LIFT)—the upward force of air that causes an object to fly

precise (pri-SISSE)—very accurate or exact

radar (RAY-dar)—a device that uses radio waves to track the location of objects

rotor (ROH-tur)—a set of rotating blades that lifts an aircraft off the ground

stealth (STELTH)—having the ability to move secretly

supersonic (soo-pur-SON-ik)—faster than the speed of sound

taper (TAY-pur)—to become narrower at one end

thrust (THRUHST)—the force that pushes a vehicle forward

vertical (VUR-tuh-kuhl)—straight up and down

READ MORE

Boothroyd, Jennifer. *How Do Helicopters Work?* Lightning Bolt Books. Minneapolis: Learner Publications Co., 2013.

Gregory, Josh. *From Birds to … Aircraft.* Innovations from Nature. Ann Arbor, Mich.: Cherry Lake Publishing, 2013.

INTERNET SITES

FactHound offers a safe, fun way to find Internet sites related to this book. All of the sites on FactHound have been researched by our staff.

Here's all you do:
Visit *www.facthound.com*
Type in this code: 9781515720362

INDEX

READ THEM ALL!

THE SCIENCE BEHIND
BATMAN'S
UNIFORM

by Agnieszka Biskup

THE SCIENCE BEHIND
BATMAN'S
GROUND VEHICLES

by Tammy Enz

THE SCIENCE BEHIND
BATMAN'S
FLYING MACHINES

by Tammy Enz

THE SCIENCE BEHIND
BATMAN'S
TOOLS

by Agnieszka Biskup